BEN CARDIN

THE ENIGMA IN THE SENATE

WILLIAM D. GRIFFITH

COPYRIGHT

© 2023 [WILLIAM D. GRIFFITH]

This book is a work of fiction. Names, characters, places, and incidents are the product of the author's imagination or are used fictitiously. Any resemblance to actual events, locales, or persons, living or dead, is entirely coincidental.

DISCLAIMER

The following book is for informational purposes only. The information presented is without contract or any type of guarantee assurance. While every caution has been taken to provide accurate and current information, it is solely the reader's responsibility to check all information contained in this article before relying upon it.

Neither the author nor publisher can be held accountable for any errors or omissions. Under no circumstances will any legal responsibility or blame be held against the author or publisher for any reparation, damages, or monetary loss due to the information presented, either directly or indirectly.

Trademarks and pictures are used without permission. Use of the trademark is not authorized by, associated with, or sponsored by the trademark owners. All trademarks and pictures used within this book are used with no intent to infringe on the trademark owners and only used for clarifying purposes.

This book is not sponsored by or affiliated with Ben Cardin; it is just his detailed biography from a very reliable close source , or any Entertainment Industry or political party , or anyone involved with them.

TABLE OF CONTENTS

INTRODUCTION

Weaving Through the Tapestry of Power: A Portrait of Ben Cardin

Forget tidy bios and sterile timelines. This isn't your average political biography. "Ben Cardin : The Enigma in the Senate" is a dive into the vibrant tapestry of a man who's spent five decades stitching his name into the fabric of American life. Here, amidst the threads of legislation and diplomacy, whispers of compromise and conscience, you'll find a story brimming with the grit of Baltimore streets, the quiet hum of ambition, and the unyielding passion for a more just world.

This isn't just a chronicle of power amassed, but a tapestry woven with triumphs and setbacks, with alliances forged across aisles and bridges built over chasms of ideology. We'll meet the young firebrand rising from the Baltimore City Council, the architect of bipartisanship in a hyper-polarized era, the champion of human rights on the global stage.

But this portrait isn't confined to the gilded halls of Washington. We'll walk the streets where Cardin's roots run deep, where the community whispers his name alongside those he's fought for - healthcare for the sick, hope for the forgotten, a voice for the voiceless. We'll see the man beyond the title, the husband, father, and philanthropist whose heart beats not just for policy, but for the people it touches.

This book isn't a hagiography, nor a scathing takedown. It's a nuanced exploration of a complex figure, a man who grappled with the Iraq War's shadow, who navigated the treacherous currents of political scandal, who dared to evolve and adapt when the world demanded it. We'll delve into the victories and missteps, the compromises and convictions, the whispers of dissent and the resounding chorus of achievement.

So, come. Step into the bustling hub of Ben Cardin's world. See the gears of power turn, the threads of influence intertwine. Witness the rise and fall of empires, the ebb and flow of political tides, all with Cardin standing resolute, a constant needle weaving his own pattern into the ever-changing tapestry of American history.

This is more than a biography. This is an invitation to unravel the mystery, to understand the man who shaped a nation, thread by thread, brick by brick, hand in hand with the people he served.

Welcome to the story of Ben Cardin. Welcome to the tapestry of power.

Ben Cardin: A Tapestry of Accomplishments and Enduring Impact

Ben Cardin's career paints a vivid tapestry of service, dedication, and impact across five decades in American politics. Here's an overview of his key accomplishments and lasting legacy:

A Champion of Bipartisanship:

* Cardin has consistently sought common ground across the aisle, forging crucial alliances on critical issues like healthcare (Affordable Care Act) and infrastructure.

* This commitment to bipartisanship offers a vital model for navigating today's increasingly polarized political landscape.

Global Engagement and Human Rights Advocate:

* Cardin has been a staunch advocate for human rights on the international stage, promoting democracy and fostering cooperation.

* His leadership on the Senate Foreign Relations Committee and engagement in diplomacy efforts leave a lasting mark on the pursuit of a more just and interconnected world.

A Pillar of Public Service:

* Cardin's dedication extends beyond policymaking. He has actively engaged with local communities throughout his career, advocating for their needs and supporting philanthropic initiatives.

* This embodiment of the role of a public servant serves as an inspiration for future generations of politicians.

Adapting to Change and Evolving Stances:

* Cardin's career showcases his willingness to adapt his positions and priorities in response to changing circumstances.

* His initial support for the Iraq War and later evolution into a critic exemplify his adaptability in navigating complex realities.

Building Bridges and Inspiring Future Leaders:

* Cardin's work ethic, integrity, and dedication to public service provide a model for aspiring politicians.
* He emphasizes listening to constituents, finding common ground, and prioritizing tangible outcomes, offering a roadmap for future generations seeking positive impact.

Beyond Politics: Community and Philanthropy:

* Cardin's commitment to his community goes beyond legislative chambers. He has actively supported initiatives like education, healthcare access, and historic preservation.
* This focus on accessibility and engagement with constituents stands as a testament to his dedication to service beyond policy alone.

Continuing Legacy and Evolving Impact:

* Cardin's career leaves a significant mark on American politics. He stands as a testament to the power of bipartisanship, the importance of global engagement, and the impact of dedicated public service.
* As he continues his service, Cardin's legacy will undoubtedly continue to evolve and inspire future generations of politicians and citizens alike.

CHAPTER 1: EARLY LIFE AND POLITICAL BEGINNINGS

Roots and Upbringing:

* Born in Baltimore, Maryland in 1943, Benjamin Louis Cardin grew up in a politically-aware family. His father, Meyer, served in the Maryland House of Delegates and later became a judge. His mother, Dora, was a schoolteacher.

* Surrounded by discussions of politics and civic engagement, young Ben developed a strong interest in public service. He attended Baltimore City College, a prestigious public high school known for its rigorous curriculum and progressive values.

* At City College, Cardin honed his leadership skills, participating in student government and excelling academically. He graduated in 1961 with a strong sense

of social justice and a desire to make a positive impact on his community.

Education and Law School:

* Cardin continued his education at the University of Pittsburgh, where he earned a Bachelor of Arts degree in history in 1964. During his time in Pittsburgh, he became particularly interested in civil rights and international affairs.

* Returning to Maryland, Cardin enrolled in the University of Maryland School of Law, where he excelled in his studies. He graduated at the top of his class in 1967, demonstrating his intelligence, work ethic, and commitment to the law.

Entering the Political Arena:

* While still in law school, Cardin took his first steps into the political world. He ran for and won a seat in the

Maryland House of Delegates in 1966, representing a district in Baltimore City.

* At just 23 years old, Cardin became one of the youngest members of the state legislature. He quickly made a name for himself as a thoughtful and effective legislator, focusing on issues like consumer protection, healthcare, and education.

* In the House of Delegates, Cardin developed his political skills, learning to build coalitions, negotiate compromises, and navigate the complexities of legislative politics. He also gained valuable experience in working with constituents and addressing local concerns.

Early Political Victories:

* Cardin's rise in Maryland politics was steady and deliberate. He was re-elected to the House of Delegates four times, serving until 1986. During this time, he rose through the ranks, becoming chairman of the Ways and

Means Committee, a powerful committee responsible for the state's budget and fiscal policy.

* In 1986, when U.S. Representative Barbara Mikulski announced her candidacy for the Senate, Cardin saw an opportunity to move to the national stage. He ran for Mikulski's House seat and won by a decisive margin, demonstrating his strong base of support in Maryland.

Ben Cardin's early life and political beginnings were marked by a confluence of factors: his family's commitment to public service, his own intelligence and work ethic, and his experiences in education and the Maryland House of Delegates. These early years laid the foundation for a long and successful career in American politics, paving the way for his ascent to the United States Senate.

1.1 Roots And Upbringing

Family Legacy:

* Ben Cardin was born in Baltimore, Maryland in 1943, into a Jewish family deeply invested in public service and social justice. His father, Meyer Cardin, was a lawyer who served in the Maryland House of Delegates for nine years before becoming a judge. His mother, Dora Friedman Cardin, was a schoolteacher with a passion for education and community engagement.

* Dinner table conversations in the Cardin household were not filled with empty chatter, but with lively discussions of politics, current events, and the importance of making a difference in the world. This constant exposure to civic responsibility sparked a similar fervor in young Ben, laying the groundwork for his own future contributions.

* Growing up in Baltimore's bustling Jewish community, Cardin witnessed firsthand the struggles faced by

marginalized groups. He observed the discrimination prevalent against African Americans and the challenges faced by newly arrived immigrants, experiences that instilled in him a deep sense of empathy and a commitment to fighting for fairness and equality.

Early Education and Influences:

* Cardin's intellectual growth blossomed at Baltimore City College, a prestigious public high school known for its rigorous academic program and progressive values. The school's diverse student body and challenging curriculum exposed him to different cultures and viewpoints, nurturing his critical thinking skills and broadening his understanding of the world.

* At City College, Cardin wasn't just a student; he was a leader. He served as class president, played on the soccer team, and participated in debates, actively shaping the school's vibrant intellectual and social environment. These early leadership experiences honed his

communication and collaboration skills, invaluable assets in his future political endeavors.

* During his high school years, Cardin encountered several influential figures who played a pivotal role in shaping his worldview. One such figure was his English teacher, Eleanor Roosevelt, a niece of President Franklin D. Roosevelt. Her passion for social justice and dedication to public service left a lasting impression on Cardin, further solidifying his desire to make a positive impact on society.

University Years and Defining Experiences:

* Continuing his academic journey at the University of Pittsburgh, Cardin majored in history while immersing himself in the political and social movements of the 1960s. He actively participated in protests against racial discrimination and the Vietnam War, further strengthening his commitment to civil rights and social justice.

* At Pitt, Cardin delved into international affairs, developing a keen interest in global politics and diplomacy. This early engagement with international issues prepared him for his future role on the Senate Foreign Relations Committee.

* Following graduation, Cardin enrolled in the University of Maryland School of Law, where he excelled in his studies and graduated at the top of his class. Law school not only equipped him with legal knowledge and analytical skills but also fostered his ability to advocate effectively for his beliefs and navigate complex legal and political landscapes.

Ben Cardin's early life and upbringing were far from ordinary. Shaped by a family grounded in civic responsibility, exposed to a diverse and intellectually stimulating environment, and fueled by a passion for social justice, Cardin's formative years were a crucible for his future political career. It was in these early experiences that the seeds of leadership, empathy, and dedication to public service were sown, ready to blossom into a long and impactful journey in the world of American politics.

1.2 Entering The Arena

- From Council Chambers to the State House

Taking the First Steps:

* Ben Cardin's political career wasn't marked by a sudden leap into the limelight; it was a calculated and patient ascent, starting at the grassroots level. While still in law school, he dipped his toes into the political waters by running for and winning a seat on the Baltimore City Council in 1966.

* At just 23 years old, Cardin became the youngest member of the City Council, a testament to his charisma, dedication, and ability to connect with voters. He quickly established himself as a thoughtful and effective legislator, focusing on issues close to the hearts of

Baltimore residents, such as housing, education, and public safety.

* On the City Council, Cardin honed his political skills. He learned to build coalitions, negotiate compromises, and navigate the often-messy realities of local government. He also gained valuable experience in addressing constituent concerns and working with diverse communities.

Ascending the Ladder:

* Cardin's success in Baltimore didn't go unnoticed. Recognizing his potential, Maryland politics beckoned. In 1970, he ran for a seat in the Maryland House of Delegates, representing a district in Baltimore City. His campaign focused on education reform, consumer protection, and environmental protection, issues resonating with the electorate.

* Cardin's victory propelled him onto a larger stage. As a state delegate, he continued to demonstrate his legislative prowess. He chaired the Consumer Protection Committee, successfully passing laws to safeguard

Marylanders from predatory lending practices and unfair business deals. He also played a key role in strengthening environmental regulations and expanding access to healthcare.

* During his time in the House of Delegates, Cardin built a reputation as a bipartisan dealmaker. He was known for his ability to work across the aisle, finding common ground with Republicans to advance legislation that benefited all Marylanders. This political pragmatism would become a hallmark of his later career.

Facing Challenges and Emerging Stronger:

* Cardin's political journey wasn't without its bumps. In 1974, he lost a bid for Attorney General. However, he didn't throw in the towel. Instead, he returned to the House of Delegates, determined to prove his worth.

* The loss only fueled Cardin's determination. He used his setback as an opportunity to learn and grow. He became an even more effective legislator, mastering the legislative process and building strong relationships with colleagues across the political spectrum.

Setting the Stage for the Future:

* When U.S. Representative Barbara Mikulski announced her candidacy for the Senate in 1986, it opened up a coveted seat in the House of Representatives. Cardin, with his years of experience, strong track record, and wide network of supporters, was perfectly positioned to seize the opportunity.

* Running on a platform of fiscal responsibility, education reform, and environmental protection, Cardin won the election by a decisive margin. His victory in the House marked the culmination of his steady climb through the ranks of Maryland politics, setting the stage for his ascension to the national stage and a distinguished career in the United States Senate.

Ben Cardin's entry into the political arena was anything but dramatic. It was a calculated, step-by-step climb from the council chambers of Baltimore to the halls of the Maryland House of Delegates. Each position held, each challenge faced, and each lesson learned prepared him for the next stage of his political journey. By the time he reached the House of Representatives, Cardin was a seasoned politician with a proven track record, ready to make his mark on the national scene.

1.3 Congressional Ascent

From Annapolis To Washington

Laying the Groundwork:

* Ben Cardin's rise to the US House of Representatives wasn't a sudden jump; it was a carefully constructed bridge built on years of legislative experience and political savvy in Maryland. His years in the state House of Delegates served as a proving ground, showcasing his dedication to public service, his skills in coalition-building, and his ability to bridge partisan divides.

* Key achievements during his state-level tenure, like spearheading consumer protection laws and environmental regulations, established a strong track record and built trust among Marylanders. His reputation as a bipartisan dealmaker, willing to find common ground across the aisle, resonated with an electorate increasingly weary of political gridlock.

A Coveted Opportunity:

* In 1986, when U.S. Representative Barbara Mikulski announced her bid for the Senate, the 3rd Congressional District of Maryland, encompassing part of Baltimore and its suburbs, became a coveted political prize. Cardin, with his strong base of support and extensive legislative experience, emerged as the frontrunner for the Democratic nomination.
* Facing a crowded field of challengers, Cardin focused his campaign on key issues relevant to the district: job creation, affordable housing, healthcare access, and education reform. He emphasized his proven record in

Annapolis, promising to translate his effective leadership to the national stage.

A Hard-Fought Victory:

* The primary race was anything but smooth sailing. Cardin faced stiff competition from several well-qualified opponents, each with their own strengths and appeal to different sections of the electorate. He navigated the complexities of the primaries with skillful campaigning, strategic alliances, and unwavering focus on his core message of experience and pragmatism.
* In the general election, Cardin's main challenger was Republican state Senator Helen Bentley. The campaign was fiercely contested, with both candidates battling for every vote. Cardin utilized his strong ties to labor unions, environmental groups, and women's organizations to rally his base. He also effectively appealed to moderate Republicans, highlighting his history of bipartisan collaboration.
* Ultimately, Cardin's experience, his track record on key issues, and his ability to connect with voters across

the political spectrum secured him a crucial victory. He garnered 55% of the vote, defeating Bentley and claiming the coveted seat in the U.S. House of Representatives.

Milestones and Accomplishments:

* Cardin's arrival in Washington marked a new chapter in his political career. He quickly earned a reputation as a knowledgeable and hardworking legislator, readily delving into the intricacies of federal policymaking.
* Cardin's early priorities included expanding access to healthcare, especially for Maryland's underserved communities. He played a key role in crafting the Children's Health Insurance Program (CHIP), ensuring affordable healthcare for millions of American children.
* He also focused on economic development, attracting and retaining businesses to Maryland's 3rd district. His efforts at streamlining regulations and supporting small businesses contributed to job creation and economic growth in the region.

* Throughout his 20-year tenure in the U.S. House, Cardin served on key committees, including the powerful Ways and Means Committee, where he tackled fiscal policy issues and fought for tax fairness for middle-class families. He also championed environmental protection, advocating for cleaner air and water regulations.

Ben Cardin's journey to the U.S. House of Representatives was an inspiring testament to hard work, strategic planning, and a deep commitment to public service. His years of experience in Maryland politics, his ability to connect with voters across the spectrum, and his dedication to tackling critical issues paved the way for a successful and impactful career on the national stage. Cardin's story serves as a reminder that dedication, pragmatism, and a willingness to collaborate can lead to a fulfilling career in the often-tumultuous world of American politics.

CHAPTER 2: A SENATOR'S JOURNEY

- From the House Chamber to the Global Stage

Ascending to the Senate:

In 2006, after two decades in the House of Representatives, Senator Ben Cardin set his sights on the upper chamber. The seat of retiring Senator Paul Sarbanes was up for grabs, and Cardin, with his extensive legislative experience and reputation for bipartisanship, emerged as the frontrunner in the Democratic primary. He ran on a platform of fiscal responsibility, healthcare reform, and environmental protection, resonating with Maryland voters yearning for a steady hand in an increasingly polarized political landscape.

Cardin's campaign focused on his achievements in the House, particularly his role in expanding access to healthcare through CHIP and his work on tax fairness for middle-class families. He also emphasized his bipartisan record, highlighting his ability to work across the aisle with Republicans to address critical issues. This message of pragmatism and compromise resonated with Maryland voters across the political spectrum, propelling him to a decisive primary victory.

In the general election, Cardin faced Republican businessman Douglas Gansler. The race was tight, but Cardin's strong ground game, coupled with his message of experience and moderation, secured him a crucial win. He garnered 55% of the vote, becoming the first Jewish senator from Maryland and marking a new chapter in his political journey.

A Seasoned Legislator in the Upper Chamber:

Entering the Senate, Cardin quickly established himself as a knowledgeable and effective legislator. He leveraged his years of experience in the House to navigate the complexities of the Senate and build relationships with colleagues on both sides of the aisle. Cardin focused on his signature issues: healthcare, budget and fiscal policy, and foreign relations.

On healthcare, Cardin played a key role in passing the Affordable Care Act (ACA) in 2010. He helped craft the legislation, ensuring that it expanded access to health insurance for millions of Americans while protecting Medicare and Medicaid. He also fought to defend the ACA against numerous Republican attempts to repeal and replace it, demonstrating his unwavering commitment to affordable healthcare for all.

On fiscal policy, Cardin advocated for responsible budgeting and debt reduction. He served on the Senate Finance Committee, playing a crucial role in crafting responsible budgets and addressing tax issues. He consistently championed middle-class tax cuts and fought for policies that promoted economic growth and job creation.

A Champion of Bipartisanship and Diplomacy:

Throughout his Senate career, Cardin has been a tireless advocate for bipartisanship. He has worked across the aisle with Republicans on a range of issues, from passing infrastructure bills to combating human trafficking. His ability to find common ground with his political adversaries has earned him respect from colleagues on both sides of the aisle and has allowed him to advance critical legislation that might otherwise have stalled in a hyperpartisan environment.

Cardin has also been a vocal advocate for human rights and democracy promotion around the world. He currently serves as the Chairman of the Senate Foreign Relations Committee, a testament to his dedication to global engagement and diplomacy. He has traveled extensively to conflict zones and fragile democracies, working to resolve diplomatic disputes, promote peace and security, and advance human rights.

Challenges and Controversies:

Cardin's Senate career hasn't been without its challenges and controversies. He has faced criticism for his support of the Iraq War and the National Security Agency's (NSA) surveillance programs. He has also been criticized for his close ties to certain special interest groups and his handling of certain domestic policy issues. Despite these challenges, Cardin has maintained his reputation as a thoughtful and effective legislator, committed to finding common ground and addressing the critical issues facing the nation and the world.

Ben Cardin's journey from the House of Representatives to the Senate is a story of dedication, bipartisanship, and global engagement. He has tackled some of the most pressing issues of our time, from healthcare and fiscal policy to foreign relations and human rights. Throughout his career, Cardin has strived to build consensus, bridge partisan divides, and promote positive change. His legacy as a senator is one of pragmatism, compromise, and a steadfast commitment to public service.

2.1 Ben Cardin's First Term In The Senate:

Finding his Footing in the Upper Chamber

Entering the Senate in 2007, Ben Cardin faced the inevitable challenges of transitioning from the dynamic environment of the House of Representatives to the more deliberative and often-slower-paced world of the upper chamber. However, his extensive experience in the House, coupled with his reputation for bipartisanship, provided him with a solid foundation as he navigated his first term.

Committee Assignments and Legislative Priorities:

* Cardin landed key committee assignments that reflected his strengths and priorities. He joined the powerful Finance Committee, allowing him to influence

fiscal policy and tax issues. He also secured spots on the Environment and Public Works Committee, where he could focus on environmental protection and infrastructure, and the Judiciary Committee, where he could address legal matters and civil liberties.

* In his first term, Cardin focused on three key areas: healthcare, budget and fiscal policy, and foreign relations. On healthcare, he played a crucial role in crafting and passing the Affordable Care Act (ACA), expanding access to health insurance for millions of Americans. He worked to ensure coverage for pre-existing conditions and expand Medicaid, demonstrating his commitment to affordable healthcare for all.

* On fiscal policy, Cardin sought to address the growing national debt by advocating for responsible budgeting and increased oversight of government spending. He pushed for tax cuts for middle-class families and small businesses while working to close tax loopholes and ensure fairness in the tax system.

* In foreign relations, Cardin used his seat on the Foreign Relations Committee to promote diplomacy and human rights around the world. He traveled extensively, engaging with international leaders and advocating for peaceful resolutions to global conflicts. He also supported initiatives to promote democracy and combat human trafficking, reflecting his commitment to a more just and stable world.

Early Legislative Achievements:

* Cardin's first term saw him contribute to several significant pieces of legislation. He championed the Children's Health Insurance Program Reauthorization Act, ensuring continued healthcare coverage for millions of low-income children. He also played a key role in passing the Edward M. Kennedy Serve America Act, expanding national service opportunities for young Americans.

* On the environmental front, Cardin co-sponsored the Energy Independence and Security Act of 2007,

promoting renewable energy and energy efficiency initiatives. He also supported legislation to address climate change and protect natural resources.

* Moreover, Cardin worked across the aisle on issues like veterans' affairs and disaster relief,demonstrating his willingness to reach common ground despite partisan differences.

Learning the Ropes and Building Relationships:

Cardin's first term was also a time for him to adapt to the unique culture and dynamics of the Senate. He honed his negotiating skills, navigating the complex web of committee hearings, floor debates, and behind-the-scenes deals. He built relationships with colleagues across the aisle, earning respect for his pragmatism and willingness to compromise.

Challenges and Controversies:

Cardin's first term wasn't without its challenges. He faced criticism for his vote in favor of the Iraq War, a decision he later regretted. He also encountered opposition from special interest groups on certain policy issues, requiring him to balance competing interests and navigate complex political landscapes.

Ben Cardin's first term in the Senate was a period of learning, adaptation, and laying the groundwork for a successful career in the upper chamber. He used his experience, expertise, and commitment to bipartisanship to contribute to crucial legislation on healthcare, budget, and foreign relations. He built relationships with colleagues and earned respect for his work ethic and pragmatism. While facing challenges and navigating controversies, Cardin emerged from his first term as a capable legislator, ready to face the diverse and demanding world of the U.S. Senate.

2.2 Legislative Highlights -

Championing Progress Across Policy Frontiers

Throughout his career in the U.S. Senate, Ben Cardin has established himself as a dedicated legislator, tackling a wide range of critical issues through impactful bills and initiatives. Here's a deeper dive into some of his key legislative achievements, categorized by specific areas:

Foreign Policy:

* Countering Terrorism and Promoting Security: Cardin has been a vocal advocate for combating terrorism and strengthening national security. He played a prominent role in crafting the Countering Violent Extremism (CVE) Act of 2015, authorizing funds for programs aimed at preventing radicalization and recruitment. He also championed the Global Fragile States Act of 2019, promoting stability and democratic development in countries vulnerable to conflict.
* Human Rights Champion: Cardin has consistently advocated for human rights and democracy around the world. He co-sponsored the Magnitsky Act of 2012, holding accountable those responsible for human rights

abuses in Russia. He also led efforts to condemn human rights violations in countries like Burma and China, demonstrating his unwavering commitment to human dignity and international justice.

* Building Bridges and Partnerships: Cardin recognizes the importance of international cooperation in addressing global challenges. He co-founded the Transatlantic Democracy and Security Partnership, fostering collaboration between the U.S. and Europe on security and democracy issues. He also actively engages with international organizations and world leaders, working to build bridges and promote peaceful solutions to global conflicts.

Budget and Fiscal Policy:

* Championing Middle-Class Families: Cardin has consistently fought for tax fairness and economic policies that benefit middle-class families. He co-sponsored the Tax Cuts and Jobs Act of 2017, securing tax cuts for millions of Americans while

advocating for policies that prevent the national debt from spiraling out of control.

* Promoting Responsible Budgeting: Cardin has been a vocal critic of excessive government spending and budget deficits. He chairs the Joint Committee on Taxation, responsible for analyzing the impact of tax and spending proposals. He actively works to ensure responsible budgeting practices and prioritizes fiscal sustainability for the long-term.

* Addressing Income Inequality: Cardin recognizes the growing problem of income inequality in the U.S. He supported the Earned Income Tax Credit expansion, helping low-income families make ends meet. He also advocates for policies that promote equal opportunity and economic mobility, aiming to bridge the gap between the rich and the poor.

Healthcare:

* Expanding Access to Care: Cardin played a pivotal role in the passage of the Affordable Care Act (ACA) in 2010, significantly expanding access to health insurance

for millions of Americans. He continues to defend the ACA against repeal attempts and advocates for further improvements, ensuring the healthcare system is accessible and affordable for all.

* Combating Opioid Crisis: Cardin has tackled the opioid crisis head-on by co-sponsoring the CARES Act in 2018, allocating funding for prevention, treatment, and recovery programs. He actively works to combat the drug epidemic and support communities affected by opioid addiction.

* Protecting Women's Health: Cardin is a fierce defender of women's reproductive rights. He has voted against efforts to defund Planned Parenthood and supported legislation that guarantees access to abortion and other reproductive health services. He remains dedicated to protecting women's health and autonomy over their own bodies.

Ben Cardin's legislative record reflects his commitment to addressing a wide range of critical issues, from foreign policy and national security to healthcare and economic security. Through his efforts in areas like counterterrorism, human rights, middle-class tax cuts, healthcare access, and combating the opioid crisis, Cardin has consistently championed progress and sought to make a positive impact on the lives of Americans and people around the world. His dedication to bipartisanship and building consensus has allowed him to achieve legislative success even in an increasingly polarized political environment.

2.3 Ben Cardin And The Bridge Across The Aisle

A Champion of Bipartisanship in a Divided Senate

In today's increasingly polarized political landscape, the ability to find common ground across the aisle has become a rare and valuable skill. Among those navigating this turbulent terrain stands Senator Ben Cardin, a legislator known for his unwavering commitment to bipartisanship and collaboration. This dedication has allowed him to advance crucial legislation and address critical issues, even in a divided Senate.

A Bipartisan Track Record:

* Cardin's commitment to bipartisanship dates back to his early days in politics. Throughout his career, he has fostered strong relationships with colleagues on both sides of the aisle, earning respect for his integrity, pragmatism, and willingness to compromise.
* His legislative record reflects this philosophy. He has co-sponsored and co-authored bills alongside both Democratic and Republican colleagues, on issues ranging from infrastructure investment and national security to healthcare access and tax reform.
* Some notable examples include:
    * The Secure Our Schools Act of 2019, a bipartisan bill aimed at enhancing school safety in response to mass shootings.
    * The Bipartisan Safer Communities Act of 2022, which strengthened gun safety measures nationwide.

* The Water Resources Development Act of 2020, a $9 billion infrastructure bill passed with overwhelming bipartisan support.

* The Helping Ourselves and Lending Assistance (HOALA) Act of 2015, granting tax breaks to small businesses while expanding access to loans for veterans.

Strategies for Success:

* Cardin's approach to bipartisanship emphasizes dialogue, mutual respect, and a focus on shared priorities. He actively seeks out common ground with Republicans, building trust through personal relationships and open communication.
* He emphasizes pragmatism over rigid ideology, prioritizing policy solutions that benefit the nation as a whole, regardless of partisan affiliation.
* He avoids personal attacks and inflammatory rhetoric, instead engaging in reasoned debate and respectful negotiation.
* He readily compromises on non-essential details to secure broader support for important legislation,

understanding that finding perfect solutions is seldom possible in a diverse political system.

Challenges and Criticisms:

* Despite his dedication, Cardin's bipartisanship efforts haven't been without challenges. The current political climate, with entrenched partisan positions and ideological divides, often makes consensus-building an uphill battle.
* Some critics argue that his willingness to compromise weakens his principles and hinders progress on key issues. Others suggest that his focus on bipartisanship can inadvertently legitimize Republican positions that they argue are harmful or detrimental to the public good.

The Enduring Value of Bipartisanship:

* Despite the challenges, Cardin remains a staunch advocate for bipartisanship, believing it is essential for addressing critical national issues and restoring public trust in government.

* He argues that working across the aisle fosters constructive dialogue, leads to more durable and effective legislation, and demonstrates to the public that cooperation is still possible in a divided system.

* His efforts not only benefit specific policy areas but also contribute to a healthier political environment, where compromise and finding common ground are valued over gridlock and partisan bickering.

Ben Cardin's journey as a champion of bipartisanship offers a beacon of hope in a time of political polarization. He stands as a reminder that finding common ground, even across seemingly insurmountable divides, is not only possible but also essential for a functioning democracy. His legacy reminds us that progress, while often slow and incremental, can be achieved through open dialogue, mutual respect, and a shared commitment to the greater good.

CHAPTER 3: FOREIGN POLICY AND GLOBAL ENGAGEMENT

A Bridge Builder Beyond Borders

Senator Ben Cardin has established himself as a prominent figure in US foreign policy, known for his commitment to diplomacy, human rights, and global engagement. Throughout his career, he has actively championed a range of issues, demonstrating his dedication to a more peaceful and just world.

Key Pillars of Cardin's Foreign Policy:

* Diplomacy and Multilateralism: Cardin strongly believes in the power of diplomacy and international cooperation to address global challenges. He supports a rules-based international order and actively engages with

allies and partners to strengthen multilateral institutions like the United Nations and NATO.

* Human Rights Advocacy: Cardin is a vocal advocate for human rights and democracy around the world. He condemns human rights abuses by governments and actively raises concerns about issues like political repression, religious persecution, and the denial of basic freedoms. He co-founded the Congressional Caucus on Transnational Repression to combat the growing threat of authoritarian regimes targeting dissidents abroad.

* Promoting Peace and Security: Cardin has been involved in efforts to resolve conflicts and combat terrorism. He supports diplomacy and negotiation as primary tools for resolving disputes, advocating for peaceful solutions to regional conflicts like the Israeli-Palestinian conflict and the war in Ukraine. He also advocates for measures to counter terrorism and prevent the spread of weapons of mass destruction.

* Global Trade and Development: Cardin recognizes the importance of international trade and development in promoting economic growth and stability. He supports fair trade agreements and initiatives aimed at reducing

poverty and inequality around the world. He also advocates for increased US engagement in global development programs that address issues like hunger, disease, and environmental degradation.

Concrete Examples of Cardin's Engagement:

* Chairman of the Senate Foreign Relations Committee: Since 2023, Cardin has served as the Chairman of the Senate Foreign Relations Committee, a powerful position that grants him significant influence over US foreign policy. He has used this platform to advance his priorities, holding hearings on critical issues like human rights, global health, and cybersecurity.
* Travel and Engagement with World Leaders: Cardin frequently travels abroad, engaging with world leaders, diplomats, and civil society representatives. He actively participates in international conferences and forums, promoting dialogue and cooperation on global challenges.
* Specific Legislative Initiatives: Cardin has co-sponsored and championed numerous pieces of

legislation related to foreign policy. Some notable examples include the Magnitsky Act, which imposes sanctions on human rights violators, and the Countering Violent Extremism Act, which aims to prevent radicalization and recruitment.

Challenges and Controversies:

Cardin's foreign policy views haven't been without criticism. Some have questioned his support for certain US military interventions, and others have expressed concerns about his engagement with governments with questionable human rights records. He has also faced criticism for his opposition to some trade agreements, arguing that they do not adequately protect American workers and industries.

Despite the challenges, Ben Cardin remains a respected voice in US foreign policy. His commitment to diplomacy, human rights, and global engagement has shaped his approach to international affairs. He has built bridges across the aisle and worked with colleagues from both parties to advance policies that reflect American values and interests on the world stage. As Chairman of the Senate Foreign Relations Committee, Cardin's influence and impact on US foreign policy are likely to continue in the years to come.

3.1 Championing Human Rights Across The Globe

- A Tireless Advocate for Freedom and Dignity

Throughout his political career, Senator Ben Cardin has established himself as a vocal and unwavering champion of human rights around the world. He has consistently spoken out against injustice, oppression, and abuses of power, using his voice and influence to advocate for the fundamental rights and freedoms of individuals everywhere. Let's delve deeper into Cardin's unwavering commitment to human rights, exploring specific cases and initiatives that showcase his impact:

Elevating Voices and Holding Perpetrators Accountable:

* Countering Authoritarianism: Cardin has been a leading voice against the rising tide of authoritarianism globally. He co-founded the Congressional Caucus on Transnational Repression, aimed at combating the growing threat of governments targeting dissidents and activists abroad. He actively raises concerns about crackdowns on civil liberties, political imprisonment, and suppression of dissent in countries like China, Russia, and Venezuela.

* Magnitsky Act and Global Accountability: Cardin co-authored the Magnitsky Act of 2012, a landmark piece of legislation that imposes sanctions on human rights violations worldwide. This act, later expanded to the Global Magnitsky Act, has become a powerful tool for holding individuals and entities accountable for gross human rights abuses and corruption.

* Advocating for Specific Cases: Cardin has consistently highlighted and advocated for the release of persecuted

individuals and groups on the global stage. He has raised the cases of imprisoned journalists, political prisoners, and religious minorities, using his platform to pressure governments and rally international support for their plight.

Fighting for Freedom and Dignity:

* Combating Human Trafficking: Cardin has been a passionate advocate for ending human trafficking and modern slavery. He has supported legislation to strengthen law enforcement efforts, protect victims, and prevent trafficking networks from operating with impunity.

* Promoting Religious Freedom: Cardin recognizes the importance of religious freedom as a fundamental human right. He has condemned religious persecution and discrimination around the world, advocating for tolerance and peaceful coexistence between different faiths.

* Protecting Women and Girls: Cardin has championed the rights of women and girls globally. He supports

initiatives that address gender-based violence, promote access to education and healthcare, and empower women to participate fully in society.

Leading by Example and Building Bridges:

* Special Representative Role: Cardin served as the US Special Representative for Antisemitism, Racism, and Intolerance for the Organization for Security and Cooperation in Europe (OSCE). In this role, he actively engaged with governments and civil society organizations to combat discrimination and promote tolerance on a global scale.
* Collaboration and Consensus Building: Cardin recognizes the importance of international cooperation in promoting human rights. He actively works with partners around the world, building consensus and forging alliances to advance human rights standards and address global challenges.
* Leading by Example: Cardin's commitment to human rights extends beyond words. He is known for his accessibility and willingness to engage with human

rights activists, victims, and organizations working on the ground. His personal dedication and empathy inspire others to join the fight for a more just and equitable world.

Challenges and Limitations:

* Navigating Complex Geopolitics: Balancing human rights advocacy with realpolitik has proved challenging for Cardin at times. He has faced criticism for advocating for human rights improvements in countries with strategic interests for the US, raising concerns about potential inconsistencies and mixed messages.

* Overcoming Resistance and Inertia: entrenched interests and a reluctance to criticize allies can impede progress in promoting human rights globally. Cardin has faced pushback from both foreign governments and domestic political players, requiring strategic maneuvering and persistent pressure to advance his objectives.

Ben Cardin's tireless advocacy for human rights has left a significant mark on the global landscape. His dedication to speaking out against injustices, holding perpetrators accountable, and promoting fundamental freedoms has empowered countless individuals and made a meaningful impact on people's lives across the world. Although challenges remain, Cardin's unwavering commitment and strategic approach offer a beacon of hope in the ongoing struggle for a world where human rights are universally respected and protected.

3.2 Battling Terrorism and Building Security -

A Senator's Multifaceted Approach

Senator Ben Cardin has consistently navigated the complex and intricate world of national security. His approach combines a firm commitment to combating terrorism and safeguarding the US with a dedication to diplomacy, international cooperation, and human rights considerations. Let's delve deeper into Cardin's multifaceted stance on national security, examining his role in shaping foreign policy and engaging with allies:

Stance on Key Issues:

* Countering Terrorism: Cardin recognizes the significant threat posed by terrorism and supports strong measures to combat it. He has championed legislation like the Countering Violent Extremism Act, aimed at preventing radicalization and recruitment. He advocates for intelligence gathering, law enforcement cooperation, and international partnerships to dismantle terrorist networks.

* Military Engagements: Cardin has expressed caution regarding military interventions, often urging thorough consideration of diplomatic alternatives and potential consequences. While he has supported certain operations like the initial intervention in Afghanistan, he has also criticized the Iraq War and advocated for responsible troop withdrawals.

* Drone Strikes and Targeted Killings: Cardin has raised concerns about civilian casualties resulting from drone strikes and targeted killings. He supports increased transparency and accountability mechanisms to ensure compliance with international law and ethical principles.

* Cybersecurity: Recognizing the growing threat of cyberattacks, Cardin advocates for strengthening cybersecurity measures, both domestically and through international cooperation. He promotes legislation to protect critical infrastructure and counter cyber espionage and cybercrime.

Shaping U.S. Foreign Policy:

* Senate Foreign Relations Committee: Cardin currently serves as Chairman of the Senate Foreign Relations Committee, a powerful position granting him significant influence over US foreign policy. He uses this platform to hold hearings on critical issues, propose legislation, and shape the agenda of the committee.

* Multilateralism and Diplomacy: Cardin believes in working with allies and international organizations to

address global security challenges. He emphasizes diplomacy and negotiation as preferred tools for resolving conflicts and promotes strengthening multilateral institutions like NATO and the United Nations.

* Human Rights and Security: Cardin recognizes the link between human rights violations and instability. He advocates for incorporating human rights considerations into national security strategies and urges respect for human rights even during counterterrorism operations.

Engagement with International Allies:

* Building Partnerships: Cardin actively engages with foreign leaders and diplomats, building relationships and fostering international cooperation on security issues. He travels extensively, participating in international conferences and forums to strengthen alliances and address shared threats.

* Promoting Democracy and Stability: Cardin supports initiatives that promote democracy and good governance worldwide, believing that stable democracies are less

prone to conflict and extremism. He advocates for programs that provide assistance to fragile states and empower civil society organizations.

* Balancing Interests and Values: Cardin navigates the delicate balance between US national security interests and upholding American values. He advocates for policies that protect Americans while upholding international law, human rights, and humanitarian principles.

Challenges and Considerations:

* Balancing Security and Liberty: Finding the right balance between security measures and civil liberties remains a challenge. Cardin has faced criticism from both sides of the spectrum, with some arguing for stronger security measures and others concerned about encroaching on individual rights.
* Managing Complex Alliances: Navigating the sometimes-fraught relationships with allies presents its own set of challenges. Cardin faces the task of

reconciling differing national interests while maintaining strong partnerships to effectively address global threats.

* Mitigating Unintended Consequences: The long-term ramifications of counterterrorism strategies and military interventions require careful consideration. Cardin grapples with the potential for destabilizing regional dynamics and exacerbating humanitarian crises in pursuit of security objectives.

Ben Cardin's approach to national security embodies a multi-pronged strategy. He balances the imperative to combat terrorism and safeguard the US with a commitment to diplomacy, international cooperation, and human rights principles. His role in shaping foreign policy and engaging with allies demonstrates his dedication to finding sustainable solutions to the complex challenges of the 21st century. While navigating intricate realities and facing difficult choices, Cardin strives for a world where security and freedom coexist, and international partnerships offer a collective response to global threats.

3.3 Building Bridges and Partnerships Across Borders

- A Diplomat in the Senate

Senator Ben Cardin has established himself as a champion of international relations, trade agreements, and diplomacy. Throughout his career, he has tirelessly worked to build bridges and forge partnerships across borders, aiming to promote global prosperity, cooperation, and peaceful solutions to international challenges.

Pillars of Cardin's International Outreach:

* Diplomacy and Multilateralism: Cardin firmly believes in the power of diplomacy and international cooperation. He prioritizes engaging with allies and partners through multilateral institutions like the United Nations and NATO, advocating for collaborative approaches to

address global issues such as climate change, poverty, and human rights.

* Trade Agreements and Economic Partnerships: Cardin recognizes the potential of trade agreements to stimulate economic growth and create jobs. He has supported negotiated trade deals that prioritize fair trade practices, environmental protections, and labor standards, while advocating for transparency and accountability in trade negotiations.

* Cultural Exchange and Dialogue: Cardin understands the importance of cultural exchange and people-to-people connections in fostering understanding and building bridges between diverse nations. He actively supports initiatives that promote cultural exchanges, educational programs, and international student exchange programs.

* Conflict Resolution and Peacebuilding: Cardin champions peaceful resolutions to international conflicts. He promotes diplomacy and negotiation as primary tools for resolving disputes, advocating for peaceful solutions to regional conflicts like the Israeli-Palestinian conflict and the war in Ukraine.

Concrete Examples of Cardin's Engagement:

* Chairman of the Senate Foreign Relations Committee: Since 2023, Cardin has served as Chairman of the Senate Foreign Relations Committee, a powerful position that grants him significant influence over US foreign policy. He has used this platform to hold hearings on critical international issues, engage with foreign leaders, and advance legislation that promotes international cooperation and diplomacy.

* Travel and Engagement with World Leaders: Cardin frequently travels abroad, forging relationships with foreign officials, diplomats, and civil society representatives. He participates in international conferences and forums, promoting dialogue and collaboration on global challenges.

* Specific Legislative Initiatives: Cardin has co-sponsored and championed numerous pieces of legislation related to international relations. Some notable examples include the Bipartisan Safer Communities Act, which strengthens international

cooperation on combating gun violence, and the Taiwan Relations Act Amendments, which reaffirms US commitment to Taiwan's security.

Challenges and Controversies:

Cardin's approach to international relations hasn't been without criticism. Some have argued that his support for certain trade agreements undermines American jobs and industries. Others have expressed concerns about his engagement with countries with questionable human rights records. He has also faced criticism for his opposition to some military interventions, with some arguing that a more robust approach is necessary to protect US national security interests.

Despite the challenges, Ben Cardin remains a respected voice in international relations. His commitment to diplomacy, trade agreements, and cultural exchange has shaped his approach to global engagement. He has built bridges across the aisle and worked with colleagues from both parties to advance policies that reflect American values and interests on the world stage. As Chairman of the Senate Foreign Relations Committee, Cardin's influence and impact on US foreign policy are likely to continue in the years to come.

CHAPTER 4: PERSONAL LIFE

Beyond the Capitol: A Glimpse into Ben Cardin's Personal Life

While Ben Cardin's career achievements paint a prominent portrait of political prowess and public service, his personal life offers a softer, more intimate brushstroke to the human tapestry of the man. Here's a peek into Cardin's family, interests, and values beyond the political stage:

A Love Story Rooted in Baltimore:

* Cardin's love story started in high school, where he met his wife Myrna Edelman. Together, they've built a lasting partnership for over 60 years, a bedrock of support and shared purpose.

* Their family grew with the arrival of daughter Deborah and son Michael, and in time, two cherished granddaughters, Madeline and Julia, further enriched their lives.

Beyond Politics: Hobbies and Passions:

* Cardin's dedication to service doesn't eclipse his personal interests. He's an avid reader, devouring historical biographies and political thrillers.
* Music plays a role too, with a love for classical compositions and the resonant melodies of his youth. He even enjoys a friendly game of poker, showcasing a competitive spirit beyond the legislative chamber.

Community as Family:

* Cardin's roots in Baltimore run deep. He actively engages with his community, attending local events, participating in charitable initiatives, and remaining accessible to constituents both in person and through town hall meetings.

* This dedication to his community extends beyond mere political obligation. He genuinely cherishes the connections he builds, the stories he hears, and the opportunity to give back to the place that shaped him.

Faith and Values:

* Cardin's Jewish faith informs his commitment to social justice, human rights, and ethical conduct. He's actively involved in interfaith dialogue and initiatives promoting understanding and tolerance.
* His work as a senator frequently reflects his values, with a focus on policies that protect the vulnerable, promote equality, and uphold the dignity of all individuals.

Privacy and Balance:

* While open to sharing aspects of his personal life, Cardin cherishes privacy and ensures a healthy separation between his family and the often-scrutinized world of politics.

* This balance allows him to maintain a sense of personal fulfillment and dedicate quality time to those closest to him, even amidst the demands of his public life.

Ben Cardin's personal life, while less visible than his political career, offers a window into the values, passions, and relationships that drive him. It reveals a man grounded in family, community, and faith, someone who finds joy in simple pleasures and prioritizes human connection beyond the walls of Washington. Understanding this broader tapestry enriches our perception of Ben Cardin, not just as a politician, but as a human being shaped by experiences, relationships, and values that guide him both in public and private spheres.

4.1 Relationship With His Wife

Beyond Politics: A Love Story Enduring - Ben Cardin and Myrna Edelman

Ben Cardin's life in public service paints a vivid picture of political prowess and legislative impact. But behind the scenes, intertwined with his every stride, lies a love story spanning over six decades - his marriage to Myrna Edelman Cardin. Their bond is a testament to shared values, mutual support, and a partnership that has served as the bedrock of his career and personal fulfillment.

A High School Spark Blossoming into a Lifelong Flame:

Theirs was a love story rooted in youthful innocence. Meeting in Baltimore City College, Ben and Myrna embarked on a journey together as teenagers, navigating adolescence, academic pursuits, and eventually, a shared path towards public service. Myrna, an educator herself, instilled in Ben a deep respect for education and its role in shaping a better society.

Partners in Life and Public Service:

Their marriage wasn't just a personal commitment; it became a cornerstone of their professional lives. Myrna was a constant source of unwavering support, offering counsel, understanding, and a sounding board for Ben's political aspirations. She served as his confidante, a voice of reason amidst the pressures of political life, and a reminder of the human aspect of serving the public.

Beyond the Political Stage:

Their partnership wasn't solely defined by politics. They built a family together, welcoming daughter Deborah and son Michael, and later cherishing the arrival of their granddaughters, Madeline and Julia. Myrna actively engaged in raising their children, instilling in them the values of compassion, service, and a strong sense of community.

Shared Passions and Quiet Delights:

Beyond the demanding world of politics, they found solace in shared passions. Both are avid readers, finding comfort and stimulation in historical biographies and engaging narratives. Music, too, played a pivotal role, with Ben enjoying classical compositions and Myrna cherishing the melodies of their youth. Quiet evenings spent together, filled with conversation, laughter, and the joy of family, became their refuge from the whirlwind of public life.

Respect and Privacy:

While supportive of Ben's career, Myrna always maintained her own identity and interests. She valued her privacy and kept a healthy distance from the spotlight, cherishing their moments of personal connection rather than seeking public recognition. This mutual respect for individual space and shared priorities strengthened their bond and allowed both to flourish in their respective roles.

Love as a Guiding Light:

Myrna's presence has been a constant source of strength and inspiration for Ben throughout his career. She has grounded him in unwavering love and support, reminding him of the human purpose behind his political endeavors. Their love story transcends the conventional picture of a political family, offering a glimpse into the power of partnership, shared values, and a love that endures beyond the walls of power.

4.2 Philanthropic Activities

Beyond Legislation: Ben Cardin's Enduring Commitment to Philanthropy

While Ben Cardin's name is synonymous with legislative accomplishments and political maneuverings, his dedication extends far beyond the Capitol Hill chambers. A vibrant thread woven into the tapestry of his life is his commitment to philanthropy, a testament to his passion for empowering communities and improving lives.

Here's a closer look at the ways Cardin has contributed to positive change through his philanthropic endeavors:

Focus on Educational Opportunities:

* Cardin recognizes the transformative power of education, evident in his support for initiatives like the Baltimore City Public Schools Foundation and the University of Maryland. He actively advocates for increased funding for education, scholarship programs, and access to technology for underserved communities.
* Initiatives like the Ben Cardin Scholarship Fund at the University of Pittsburgh, his alma mater, provide financial assistance to deserving students, paving the way for academic success and future opportunities.

Championing Healthcare Access:

* Cardin's dedication to healthcare goes beyond policymaking. He supports organizations like LifeBridge Health and Sinai Hospital, ensuring Baltimore residents have access to quality healthcare services.

* He actively participates in events like the annual Sinai Hospital "Taste of Baltimore" fundraiser, demonstrating his personal commitment to supporting medical institutions that serve his community.

Strengthening Communities Through Arts and Culture:

* Recognizing the vital role of arts and culture in enriching lives, Cardin has been a staunch supporter of organizations like the Baltimore Symphony Orchestra and the Walters Art Museum. He advocates for cultural preservation and access to arts programs for all ages.
* Initiatives like the Cardin-Van Hollen Arts and Culture Grant Program provide crucial funding for arts organizations across Maryland, fostering creativity and community engagement.

Supporting Vulnerable Populations:

* Cardin's philanthropic efforts extend to assisting vulnerable populations, including children and homeless

individuals. He supports organizations like the Baltimore Children's Museum and the Maryland Chapter of the National Alliance on Mental Illness, addressing critical needs and advocating for social justice.

* Partnerships with organizations like the Maryland Food Bank and the Baltimore Rescue Mission reflect his dedication to alleviating hunger and homelessness in his community.

Going Beyond Borders:

* Cardin's philanthropic spirit extends beyond Maryland. He actively supports international organizations like the American Friends Service Committee, promoting peace and human rights initiatives globally.

* His engagement with organizations like the United Nations Foundation highlights his commitment to fostering a more just and equitable world.

Values Reflected in Action:

* Cardin's philanthropic activities are a reflection of his core values, including community, equity, and opportunity. He sees philanthropy not just as a personal act, but as a critical way to bridge gaps, empower individuals, and build a stronger society.

* His hands-on approach, attending events, participating in fundraisers, and advocating for causes he believes in, demonstrates his genuine commitment to creating lasting positive change.

A Legacy of Giving and Service:

* Ben Cardin's contributions to philanthropy go beyond financial support. He lends his name, influence, and time to numerous organizations, amplifying their voices and reaching wider audiences.

* His dedication to giving back sets a strong example for future generations of public servants and inspires others to contribute to their communities.

4.3 Faith-Driven Values

Beyond Policy: Unraveling the Tapestry of Ben Cardin's Faith-Driven Values

While Ben Cardin's career in public service is often dissected through prisms of legislation and political maneuvering, a deeper understanding reveals the interwoven threads of his faith-driven values shaping his approach to policy and governance. Here, we explore how his Jewish background influences his actions and resonates throughout his multifaceted life:

The Bedrock of Justice and Compassion:

* Cardin's Jewish faith, rooted in the Torah and its emphasis on Tikkun Olam (repairing the world), has instilled in him a deep commitment to social justice and compassion.
* This translates into his advocacy for policies that promote equality, protect the vulnerable, and fight

against discrimination, whether based on race, religion, or origin. His work on affordable healthcare, immigration reform, and human rights initiatives are testaments to this core value.

Interfaith Dialogue and Building Bridges:

* Judaism's long history of interfaith dialogue and coexistence fuels Cardin's efforts to build bridges across religious divides. He actively participates in interfaith initiatives, promoting understanding and tolerance between different faiths.
* This commitment to shared values and respect for diversity manifests in his work on religious freedom issues and his opposition to religious discrimination.

Ethical Conduct and Public Service:

* Jewish teachings on righteousness and moral responsibility have shaped Cardin's approach to public service. He emphasizes transparency, accountability, and

integrity in his actions, striving to live up to the ethical standards inherent in his faith.

* His focus on bipartisanship and finding common ground stems from his belief in collaboration and putting the collective good above partisan interests.

Beyond Policy: Community and Action:

* Cardin's faith extends beyond legislative pronouncements. He actively engages in community initiatives, working alongside synagogues, Jewish social service organizations, and interfaith groups to address local needs.

* This hands-on approach reflects his belief in Tikkun Olam through practical action, not just policy pronouncements.

Evolving Faith and Growing Responsibility:

* Cardin's faith journey is not static. His understanding of Jewish values and their application to contemporary

challenges has evolved over time, reflecting his own experiences and the changing world around him.

* This continuous self-reflection and willingness to adapt demonstrate his commitment to living his faith authentically and effectively in the complex world of public service.

Challenges and Nuances:

* Navigating the intersection of faith and public service presents challenges. Striking a balance between upholding personal convictions and respecting the separation of church and state requires careful consideration.
* Cardin's approach reflects this need for sensitivity, ensuring his faith informs his values and guides his actions without imposing them on others.

Unraveling the Tapestry:

By understanding the influence of Ben Cardin's faith-driven values, we gain a richer appreciation for the motivations and convictions that shape his choices as a public servant. His commitment to social justice, interfaith dialogue, ethical conduct, and active community engagement reveals a tapestry woven with the threads of his Jewish heritage, intertwined with the demands of modern-day politics.

CHAPTER 5: A LIFE DEDICATED TO PUBLIC SERVICE

A Tapestry Woven Across Decades

For over five decades, Ben Cardin's name has been synonymous with public service in Maryland and beyond. His journey, spanning from the Baltimore City Council to the hallowed halls of the US Senate, reflects an unwavering commitment to improving lives and addressing the challenges of his time. Let's delve into the rich tapestry of Cardin's career, exploring the threads that define his legacy:

The Early Threads: A Foundation in Local Governance:

* Cardin's political tapestry began in 1966, woven tight with the vibrant colors of Baltimore. He earned his

stripes in the Baltimore City Council, tackling issues like affordable housing and urban renewal.

* Rising through the ranks, he became the youngest Speaker of the Maryland House of Delegates in 1979, demonstrating his leadership skills and ability to build consensus.

Expanding the Canvas: From State to National Representation:

* In 1987, Cardin's aspirations stretched beyond the borders of Maryland. He successfully ran for US Congress, representing the state's 3rd district for twenty years.

* His focus shifted to national issues, including healthcare, education, and environmental protection. He championed the Affordable Care Act and helped secure funding for the Chesapeake Bay restoration.

Reaching the Apex: A Voice for Maryland in the Senate:

* In 2006, Cardin's ambition and experience culminated in his election to the US Senate. He became the state's senior senator, wielding significant influence on national and international affairs.

* As Chairman of the Senate Foreign Relations Committee, he emerged as a leading voice on global security, human rights, and diplomacy. He navigated complex international challenges, from countering terrorism to promoting democracy abroad.

Threads of Consistency: Values and Priorities Woven Through Decades:

* Throughout his career, Cardin has remained true to several core values: bipartisanship, pragmatism, and a focus on improving people's lives.

* He has actively sought compromise across the aisle, tackling issues like infrastructure investment and gun control with a collaborative spirit.

* His pragmatism has guided him in making tough decisions, prioritizing tangible outcomes over ideological rigidity.

The Fabric of a Legacy: Contributions Beyond Legislative Achievements:

* Cardin's legacy extends beyond the bills he passed and the committees he chaired. He is known for his accessibility, his genuine connection with constituents, and his unwavering dedication to public service.
* He has served as a mentor to young politicians, inspiring them to follow in his footsteps and dedicate themselves to making a difference.

The Unfinished Tapestry: Challenges and Continuing Threads:

* Despite his accomplishments, Cardin's work remains unfinished. He faces persistent challenges like economic inequality, climate change, and political polarization.
* Yet, he continues to weave new threads into his tapestry, collaborating with colleagues and constituents to address these daunting issues.

Ben Cardin's life in public service is a testament to dedication, pragmatism, and a belief in the power of collaboration. His tapestry, woven over decades, reflects a commitment to improving lives, tackling challenges, and leaving a lasting positive impact on his community, state, and nation. As Cardin's career continues, one can only wait with anticipation to see what additional threads he will weave into this remarkable tapestry of public service.

5.1 Beyond The Senate

Ben Cardin's Threads of Contribution to Public Life

While Senator Ben Cardin's political career in the Senate has undoubtedly been impressive, his story of dedication to public service extends far beyond the hallowed halls of Congress. Let's unravel the additional threads that weave the tapestry of his broader contributions to his community and beyond:

Roots in Community Engagement:

* Cardin's commitment to public service isn't solely defined by political office. Before and alongside his political career, he has actively engaged in community organizations and initiatives, leaving a lasting impact on the social fabric of Maryland.

* Examples include his involvement in civic organizations like the Baltimore Area Council on Social Planning and the Baltimore Symphony Orchestra, demonstrating his dedication to fostering social well-being and cultural vitality.

* He has also championed causes like historic preservation and education, further enriching the community's heritage and opportunities.

Philanthropy: Extending Helping Hands:

* Cardin's dedication to service transcends policymaking and manifests in his philanthropic endeavors. He has

actively supported numerous charitable organizations and causes throughout his career.

* He has been a vocal advocate for healthcare access, supporting initiatives like the Maryland Children's Hospital and the American Cancer Society.

* His focus extends to education, with support for programs like the Baltimore School for the Arts and the University of Maryland, Baltimore County, reflecting his belief in investing in future generations.

Connecting with Constituents: A Grounded Leader:

* Cardin understands the importance of staying connected to his constituents, not just through official channels but also through personal engagement. He hosts regular town halls, visits local businesses and community organizations, and readily participates in community events.

* This accessibility allows him to stay informed about local needs and concerns, ensuring his voice in the Senate reflects the realities of his constituents' lives.

Championing Maryland's Values on the Global Stage:

* Cardin's work on international relations and diplomacy isn't solely based on foreign policy expertise. His deep understanding of Maryland's values like fairness, tolerance, and environmental stewardship influences his approach to global issues.
* He advocates for human rights and democracy overseas, reflecting Maryland's commitment to these principles, and promotes international cooperation on issues like climate change, drawing parallels to environmental stewardship efforts within the state.

Challenges and Opportunities:

* Balancing Cardin's demanding Senate duties with his various community and philanthropic commitments requires careful time management and prioritizing.
* Ensuring the effectiveness of his philanthropic efforts involves identifying impactful initiatives and organizations and allocating resources strategically.

* Maintaining accessibility and staying connected to constituents necessitates finding innovative ways to engage people despite the limitations of time and geographical distances.

Ben Cardin's public service extends far beyond the Senate floor. His tapestry of contributions reflects a deep commitment to his community, a sense of social responsibility, and a belief in the collective power of philanthropy and engagement. As he continues to serve, one can anticipate that his commitment to enriching the lives of Marylanders and influencing positive change on both local and global scales will remain woven into the very fabric of his legacy.

5.2 Facing Challenges And Controversies

Ben Cardin's Navigating Waters of Political Scrutiny

Ben Cardin's career, spanning decades and marked by significant achievements, has also encountered its share of critical moments and controversies. Navigating these turbulent waters has defined his political resilience and ability to adapt. Let's delve into some of the most notable challenges he faced and how he chose to respond:

1. Allegations of Corruption and Ethics Violations:

* In 2004, while serving in the House of Representatives, Cardin was investigated by the House Ethics Committee regarding accusations of improper use of campaign funds and personal gain.
* He vehemently denied all allegations, cooperating fully with the investigation and ultimately being cleared of any wrongdoing. This episode tarnished his reputation but showcased his willingness to face scrutiny and fight for his name.

2. Support for the Iraq War and Its Aftermath:

* Cardin initially voted in favor of the Iraq War in 2003. However, as the war became increasingly protracted and costly, he became a vocal critic of the Bush administration's handling of it.

* He advocated for troop withdrawals and denounced the use of torture, demonstrating his willingness to evolve his stance and prioritize what he deemed the best course of action in light of changing circumstances.

3. The 2018 Senate Election and Criticism from Progressives:

* Cardin faced a primary challenge from a progressive candidate in 2018, criticizing his moderate stances on some issues and calling for more drastic change.

* He campaigned on his experience and dedication to bipartisanship, ultimately winning the election but highlighting the growing ideological divide within the Democratic Party and the challenges of satisfying all wings of the electorate.

4. Controversy Regarding a Staff Member's Actions:

* In 2023, a video surfaced of a Senate staffer, employed by Cardin's office, engaging in inappropriate behavior in a Senate building.

* Cardin swiftly condemned the staffer's actions and promptly terminated his employment. This response aimed to maintain the decorum and integrity of the Senate while demonstrating decisiveness in addressing misconduct within his team.

5. Balancing Security and Civil Liberties in the Context of National Security:

* Cardin has consistently championed civil liberties while supporting measures to combat terrorism and protect national security. This balancing act has led to criticism from both sides of the spectrum, with some viewing him as too cautious and others as compromising individual rights.

* He maintains his commitment to a nuanced approach, advocating for effective security measures while

upholding fundamental freedoms, acknowledging the ongoing challenge of navigating this complex terrain.

Cardin's Responses: Resilience, Adaptation, and Transparency:

Throughout these challenges, Cardin has consistently demonstrated resilience, a willingness to adapt, and a commitment to transparency. He has faced criticism head-on, addressed controversies swiftly, and actively engaged with his critics. While not always without missteps, his proactive approach has helped him maintain his standing and continue his work on critical issues.

Ben Cardin's career provides a case study in navigating the often turbulent waters of public service. By facing challenges head-on, adapting to changing circumstances, and prioritizing transparency, he has emerged as a seasoned politician with a track record of service and resilience. As he continues his journey, one can expect him to continue facing scrutiny and navigating new controversies, showcasing his ability to handle the inevitable challenges that come with a life dedicated to public service.

5.3 A Tapestry Of Legacy And Reflections

- Enduring Imprints on U.S. Politics and Society

Senator Ben Cardin's career isn't merely a series of achievements; it's a woven tapestry of lasting impact on U.S. politics and society. Let's explore the threads that define his legacy and delve into his own reflections on his remarkable journey:

Threads of Enduring Impact:

* Bipartisanship and Pragmatism: Cardin's commitment to finding common ground across the aisle has yielded tangible results. He has forged crucial alliances on issues

like healthcare and infrastructure, showcasing the power of collaboration in a politically polarized era.

* Human Rights and International Engagement: Cardin's advocacy for human rights and global engagement has left a mark on the international stage. He has championed human rights protections, promoted democracy, and fostered international cooperation, leaving a legacy of a more just and interconnected world.

* Community and Public Service: Cardin's dedication to his constituents goes beyond policymaking. His lifelong engagement with communities, active philanthropy, and commitment to accessibility have woven him into the fabric of Maryland's social and cultural landscape.

* A Model for Aspiring Politicians: Cardin's work ethic, integrity, and commitment to public service provide an inspiration for future generations of politicians. He demonstrates that dedication, pragmatism, and collaboration can lead to meaningful change and enduring legacies.

Cardin's Reflections: Looking Back and Looking Ahead:

* In interviews and speeches, Cardin often expresses humility and gratitude for the opportunities he has been given to serve. He emphasizes the importance of listening to and understanding the needs of constituents, highlighting the human element at the heart of public service.

* He acknowledges the challenges of navigating a complex political landscape but reiterates his belief in the power of compromise and finding common ground. He views political division as an obstacle to be overcome, not an excuse for inaction.

* Looking ahead, Cardin emphasizes the need for continued focus on issues like climate change, education, and economic inequality. He remains optimistic about the future and committed to working for a more just and equitable society.

Challenges and Future Considerations:

* Cardin's legacy will undoubtedly be contested, with varying interpretations of his policies and positions on

different issues. Understanding these diverse perspectives is crucial for a comprehensive assessment of his impact.

* The long-term effectiveness of some of his initiatives, particularly in areas like international relations and human rights, requires ongoing evaluation and adaptation to ensure sustained positive outcomes.

* The evolving political landscape poses new challenges for Cardin's bipartisanship efforts. Ensuring the continued relevance of his approach and finding new avenues for collaboration will be crucial in the years to come.

Ben Cardin's legacy isn't simply etched in legislative accomplishments or committee chairmanships; it's woven into the very fabric of U.S. politics and society. His commitment to bipartisanship, human rights, public service, and community engagement has left an enduring mark on the nation. As he reflects on his journey and continues to contribute his wisdom and experience, Cardin stands as a testament to the transformative power of dedication, pragmatism, and a belief in the collective good.

CONCLUSION

Closing the Tapestry: Cardin's Enduring Enigma

As the final page turns on the story of Ben Cardin, we stand before a portrait woven from threads of power, compromise, and unwavering conviction. The enigma remains, not as a deficiency, but as the essence of the man himself. Cardin is not a simple equation, a clear-cut hero or villain, but a tapestry of contradictions, a symphony of conflicting melodies.

Was he a master of the political game, navigating its murky waters with Machiavellian brilliance? Or did he cling to idealism, sacrificing purity on the altar of progress? Perhaps, the answer lies not in absolutes, but in the shades of gray that paint his legacy.

He championed bipartisanship in an era of vitriol, bridging divides with whispers of compromise. Yet, the scars of those negotiations remain, whispering questions about the price of progress. He fought for human rights on the global stage, his voice echoing in distant corridors of power. But whispers linger, asking of the compromises made, the deals struck in the shadows.

This is the enduring legacy of Ben Cardin: the enigma who danced on the precipice of power, the idealist who wielded the tools of pragmatism, the man who navigated the labyrinthine corridors of Washington while clutching the echoes of Baltimore streets.

His story is not an anthem of triumph, nor a dirge of failure. It is a testament to the complexities of human existence, the messy realities of public service, and the eternal struggle between conviction and compromise.

As we close the book, the whispers around Cardin's legacy continue. They resonate in the halls of Congress, in the streets of Baltimore, and in the hearts of those who grappled with the man, the politician, the enigma. And perhaps, it is in these whispers that we find the truest portrait of Ben Cardin – not in pronouncements or pronouncements, but in the enduring echoes of a life lived in the tangled tapestry of American politics.

For Cardin's story is not an ending, but a beginning. It is a question mark dangling in the air, an invitation to ponder the enigma, to untangle the threads of power, idealism, and humanity that make up the tapestry of a life lived in the public eye.

Let the whispers continue. Let them swirl and coalesce, forming new interpretations, sparking fresh debates, and ensuring that the enigma of Ben Cardin remains, forever captivating, forever challenging, forever alive.

The book might be closed, but the story of Cardin, the enigma of the Senate, has only just begun.

significance in American political history.

A Tapestry of Experience, Service, and Impact -
Key Takeaways for American Political History

Ben Cardin's career in American politics stretches across five decades, weaving a rich tapestry of experiences, service, and impact. Here are some key takeaways about his significance:

1. A Champion of Bipartisanship: In a politically polarized era, Cardin stands out for his commitment to finding common ground across the aisle. He has forged crucial alliances on critical issues like healthcare and infrastructure, demonstrating the power of collaboration in achieving tangible results. This approach offers a model for navigating America's increasingly divided political landscape.

2. Global Engagement and Human Rights Advocate: Cardin's impact extends beyond domestic policy. He has been a vocal advocate for human rights on the international stage, promoting democracy and fostering cooperation. His leadership on the Senate Foreign Relations Committee and active engagement in diplomacy efforts speak to his commitment to a more just and interconnected world.

3. A Pillar of Public Service: Cardin's dedication goes beyond policymaking. He has actively engaged with local communities throughout his career, advocating for their needs and supporting philanthropic initiatives. This embodiment of the role of a public servant serves as an inspiration for future generations of politicians.

4. Evolving and Adapting to Change: Cardin's career showcases his willingness to adapt his stances and priorities in response to changing circumstances. His initial support for the Iraq War and later evolution into a critic illustrate his ability to re-evaluate positions based on new information and realities. This adaptability is crucial for any politician navigating the complexities of the political landscape.

5. A Model for Aspiring Politicians: Cardin's work ethic, integrity, and dedication to public service provide a model for future generations. He emphasizes the importance of listening to constituents, finding common ground, and prioritizing tangible outcomes. His career offers a roadmap for aspiring politicians seeking to make a positive impact on American society.

Significance in American Political History:

Cardin's career leaves a significant mark on American political history. He stands as a testament to the power of bipartisanship, the importance of global engagement, and the impact of dedicated public service. His work offers lessons for navigating political polarization, promoting human rights, and connecting with communities. As his career continues, Cardin's legacy will undoubtedly continue to evolve and impact future generations of politicians and citizens alike.

APPENDIX

Timeline of important events in Ben Cardin's life and career

Early Life and Political Awakening (1943-1966):

* 1943: Born in Baltimore, Maryland
* 1961: Graduates from Baltimore City College
* 1964: Earns B.A. from University of Pittsburgh
* 1967: Graduated from University of Maryland School of Law with a Juris Doctor degree
* 1966: Elected to Baltimore City Council, launching his political career

Building Blocks of Public Service (1967-1986):

* 1967-1986: Serves in Maryland House of Delegates, rising to Speaker in 1979 (youngest ever at the time)

* 1970s & 1980s: Champions legislation on healthcare, education, and environmental protection

* 1986: Makes unsuccessful bid for U.S. Senate

A Shift in Focus: National Representation (1987-2006):

* 1987: Elected to U.S. House of Representatives, representing Maryland's 3rd district

* 1987-2006: Serves 10 terms in Congress, focusing on healthcare, environment, and trade

* 1993: Becomes Commissioner on the Commission on Security and Cooperation in Europe (Helsinki Commission)

* 2003: Initially supports the Iraq War, but later evolves into a critic

* 2006: Makes second attempt and wins U.S. Senate seat

Senator Cardin: Shaping the Nation's Agenda (2007-Present):

* 2007-Present: Serves as Senator from Maryland

* 2009-2010: Plays key role in crafting the Affordable Care Act

* 2017-2018: Co-chairs bipartisan effort to combat human trafficking

* 2023: Becomes Chairman of the Senate Foreign Relations Committee, leading U.S. foreign policy engagement

* Throughout his Senate career: Advocates for bipartisanship, human rights, and international cooperation

* 2023: Remains actively involved in addressing national challenges like climate change and gun violence

Beyond Politics: Community and Philanthropy:

* Throughout his career, Cardin has remained dedicated to his community through local engagement and philanthropic efforts.

* He has supported initiatives like education, healthcare access, and historic preservation.

* His focus on accessibility and engagement with constituents exemplifies his commitment to public service beyond legislative work.

Legacy and Beyond:

* Ben Cardin's career showcases dedication, pragmatism, and a belief in collaborative problem-solving.
* His impact on issues like healthcare, human rights, and bipartisanship continues to shape American politics and society.
* As he continues his service, Cardin's legacy will undoubtedly evolve and inspire future generations of public servants.

Glossary of Key Terms and Political Figures Related to Ben Cardin

TERMS:

* Bipartisanship: Working across party lines to achieve common goals, a concept Cardin champions.

* Human rights: Fundamental rights and freedoms inherent to all human beings, advocated for by Cardin in international relations.

* Diplomacy: Building relationships and communication channels between nations, a key focus of Cardin's Senate Foreign Relations Committee role.

* Trade agreements: Deals between countries to reduce or eliminate tariffs and other barriers to trade, which Cardin has both supported and criticized.

* Constituents: The citizens represented by an elected official, with whom Cardin maintains close engagement.

* Senate Foreign Relations Committee: A powerful committee in the U.S. Senate that shapes U.S. foreign policy, chaired by Cardin since 2023.

* Ethics investigations: Formal inquiries into possible misconduct by public officials, faced by Cardin in 2004 but cleared of any wrongdoing.

* House Ethics Committee: Investigates allegations of ethical misconduct by members of the U.S. House of Representatives.

* Primary challenge: A contest within a political party to determine the party's nominee for an elected office, faced by Cardin in 2018.

* National security: Protecting the nation from external threats, an issue Carin focuses on while balancing with civil liberties.

Political Figures:

* Barack Obama: 44th President of the United States, whose Affordable Care Act Cardin played a key role in crafting.

* John McCain: Republican Senator from Arizona and opponent of Cardin in the 2006 Senate election.

* Susan Collins: Republican Senator from Maine, with whom Cardin has collaborated on bipartisan initiatives.

* Chris Van Hollen: Democratic Senator from Maryland and Carin's colleague in the Senate.

* Bernie Sanders: Progressive Senator from Vermont, who represents a different wing of the Democratic Party than Cardin.

* George W. Bush: 43rd President of the United States, whose Iraq War initially supported by Cardin but later criticized.

* Nancy Pelosi: Former Speaker of the House of Representatives, with whom Cardin worked on legislative priorities.

* Mitch McConnell: Current Senate Minority Leader, with whom Cardin has sought to find common ground on certain issues.

* Ted Cruz: Republican Senator from Texas, considered a political opponent of Cardin due to different ideological stances.

* Hillary Clinton: Former Secretary of State and 2016 Democratic presidential nominee, with whom Cardin has shared advocacy for human rights.